AF454154

I AM A SUCCESS ~~Failure~~ Journey FOR BOSS LADIES

By Tra-C J Pierce

Hello, Boss Lady!

Thank you for your purchase. I am so glad you will take this journey with me. You and I have like minds. We both are in pursuit of something big. There are millions of women who share our passion. While we are on this journey, let's dive in deep and go after this with every ounce of passion that God has given us. I believe we can command the universe and it will respond because it doesn't discriminate. It responds to those who are desperate and determined. It responds to those Boss Ladies who will not stop until they get what they want. That's us, so Let's Go!

Tra-C

Act Like A Boss By....

What is your passion?
Name three things you are passionate about

Decide if you can turn your passion into profit

1.________________________   ☐ Yes   ☐ No

2.________________________   ☐ Yes   ☐ No

3.________________________   ☐ Yes   ☐ No

My goal for today is?

____

____

____

Bossy Thought:
I HAVE THE POWER TO SUCCEED.

Being accountable and keeping track of your activates is very important while you are on this journey. Becoming a Boss Lady is hard work, and it will not happen overnight, but it will happen. Please journal thoughts about the activities you experience today.

ACT LIKE A BOSS BY....

DO YOU REALLY HAVE WHAT IT TAKES?
EXPLAIN BELOW WHY OR WHY NOT

TICK BOX YES OR NO DO YOU HAVE WHAT IT TAKES?

_______________________________   ☐ YES   ☐ NO

_______________________________   ☐ YES   ☐ NO

_______________________________   ☐ YES   ☐ NO

MY GOAL FOR TODAY IS?

____

____

____

BOSSY THOUGHT:
I BELIEVE IN MYSELF.

ACT LIKE A BOSS BY....

WHAT WILL YOUR MAIN FOCUS BE?

TICK BOX YES OR NO

CUSTOMER SERVICE ☐ YES   ☐ NO

QUALITY ☐ YES   ☐ NO

QUANTITY ☐ YES   ☐ NO

MY GOAL FOR TODAY IS?

____

____

____

BOSSY THOUGHT:
I WILL SOAR ON EAGLE WINGS.

Being accountable and keeping track of your activates is very important while you are on this journey. Becoming a Boss Lady is hard work, and it will not happen overnight, but it will happen. Please journal thoughts about the activities you experience today.

ACT LIKE A BOSS BY....

HOW MUCH TIME CAN YOU COMMIT TO GROWING YOUR BUSINESS?

HOURS/DAY

DAYS/WK

MY GOAL FOR TODAY IS?

BOSSY THOUGHT:
I AM IN CONTROL OF MY DESTINY.

Being accountable and keeping track of your activates is very important while you are on this journey. Becoming a Boss Lady is hard work, and it will not happen overnight, but it will happen. Please journal thoughts about the activities you experience today.

ACT LIKE A BOSS BY....

DECIDE ON A BUSINESS—

WHAT BUSINESS DID YOU DECIDE ON?

____

____

WHY DID YOU CHOOSE THIS BUSINESS?

____

MY GOAL FOR TODAY IS?

____

____

____

BOSSY THOUGHT:
I SPEAK THE WORD OF LIFE.

ACT LIKE A BOSS BY....

WHAT IS YOUR FAVORITE QUOTE?

____

____

WHY DID YOU SELECT THIS QUOTE?

____

____

MY GOAL FOR TODAY IS?

____

____

____

BOSSY THOUGHT:
I AM MORE THAN A CONQUER.

Being accountable and keeping track of your activates is very important while you are on this journey. Becoming a Boss Lady is hard work, and it will not happen overnight, but it will happen. Please journal thoughts about the activities you experience today.

"It's OK to make a D-Dream, Drive, Deliver."

Act Like A Boss By....

Choosing a mentor -

Who is your mentor?
____

Why did you choose this person?
____

____

What is their experience?
____

My goal for today is?

____

____

____

Bossy Thought:
The universe responds to me.

Being accountable and keeping track of your activates is very important while you are on this journey. Becoming a Boss Lady is hard work, and it will not happen overnight, but it will happen. Please journal thoughts about the activities you experience today.

ACT LIKE A BOSS BY....

CHOOSE A BUSINESS COACH CHECK OUR SCORE

VISIT: WWW.SCORE.ORG

WHAT DO YOU THINK ABOUT THE SCORE AND THE SERVICES OFFERED?

MY GOAL FOR TODAY IS?

BOSSY THOUGHT:
I AM A PASSIONATE PERSON.

BEING ACCOUNTABLE AND KEEPING TRACK OF YOUR ACTIVATES IS VERY IMPORTANT WHILE YOU ARE ON THIS JOURNEY. BECOMING A BOSS LADY IS HARD WORK, AND IT WILL NOT HAPPEN OVERNIGHT, BUT IT WILL HAPPEN. PLEASE JOURNAL THOUGHTS ABOUT THE ACTIVITIES YOU EXPERIENCE TODAY.

ACT LIKE A BOSS BY....

RESEARCH

What industry is your business apart of?

Do some research on your industry?

My goal for today is?

BOSSY THOUGHT:
I AM A RESOURCEFUL PERSON.

Act Like A Boss By....

RESEARCH – Perform market research:

Is your business unique?

____

Is there a strong vacancy for your business to thrive?

____

Is there a void in the market place for your unique business?

____

My goal for today is?

____

____

____

Bossy Thought:
People seek my advice.

Being accountable and keeping track of your activates is very important while you are on this journey. Becoming a Boss Lady is hard work, and it will not happen overnight, but it will happen. Please journal thoughts about the activities you experience today.

____

____

____

____

____

____

____

____

____

____

____

____

____

____

____

____

____

____

____

____

____

____

____

____

____

____

____

____

ACT LIKE A BOSS BY....

RESEARCH – PERFORM MARKET RESEARCH:

ARE YOU A MINORITY OWNED BUSINESS OWNER? ☐ YES ☐ NO

GET CERTIFIED! VISIT: HTTPS://WWW.MWBE-ENTERPRISES.COM/

NOTES:

MY GOAL FOR TODAY IS?

BOSSY THOUGHT:
I AM A GREAT LEADER.

BEING ACCOUNTABLE AND KEEPING TRACK OF YOUR ACTIVATES IS VERY IMPORTANT WHILE YOU ARE ON THIS JOURNEY.
BECOMING A BOSS LADY IS HARD WORK, AND IT WILL NOT HAPPEN OVERNIGHT, BUT IT WILL HAPPEN. PLEASE
JOURNAL THOUGHTS ABOUT THE ACTIVITIES YOU EXPERIENCE TODAY.

ACT LIKE A BOSS BY....

RESEARCH- WHO'S YOUR FAVORITE BUSINESSWOMAN?

WHO IS SHE OPRAH WINFREY? ☐ YES ☐ NO

WHAT DOES SHE DO?

WHAT IS HER NET WORTH? - $

WHAT INSPIRES YOU ABOUT HER?

MY GOAL FOR TODAY IS?

BOSSY THOUGHT:
I CAN BECAUSE I BELIEVE I CAN.

Being accountable and keeping track of your activates is very important while you are on this journey. Becoming a Boss Lady is hard work, and it will not happen overnight, but it will happen. Please journal thoughts about the activities you experience today.

ACT LIKE A BOSS BY.....

RESEARCH— WHO'S YOUR FAVORITE BUSINESSWOMAN?

WHO IS SHE IRENE ROSENFELD? ☐ YES ☐ NO

WHAT DOES SHE DO?

WHAT IS HER NET WORTH? - $

WHAT INSPIRES YOU ABOUT HER?

MY GOAL FOR TODAY IS?

BOSSY THOUGHT:
I WILL NOT SPEAK DEFEAT.

Act Like A Boss By....

RESEARCH – WHO'S YOUR FAVORITE BUSINESSWOMAN?

WHO IS SHE CAROL M. MEYROWITZ? ☐ YES ☐ NO

WHAT DOES SHE DO? _______________

WHAT IS HER NET WORTH? – $ _______________

WHAT INSPIRES YOU ABOUT HER? _______________

My goal for today is?

____

____

____

BOSSY THOUGHT:
I WILL USE MY POWERWORDS.

BEING ACCOUNTABLE AND KEEPING TRACK OF YOUR ACTIVATES IS VERY IMPORTANT WHILE YOU ARE ON THIS JOURNEY. BECOMING A BOSS LADY IS HARD WORK, AND IT WILL NOT HAPPEN OVERNIGHT, BUT IT WILL HAPPEN. PLEASE JOURNAL THOUGHTS ABOUT THE ACTIVITIES YOU EXPERIENCE TODAY.

ACT LIKE A BOSS BY....

RESEARCH – WHO'S YOUR FAVORITE BUSINESSWOMAN?

WHO IS SHE INDRA NOOYI? ☐ YES ☐ NO

WHAT DOES SHE DO?

WHAT IS HER NET WORTH? - $

WHAT INSPIRES YOU ABOUT HER?

MY GOAL FOR TODAY IS?

BOSSY THOUGHT:
I ENVISION WHAT I WANT IN LIFE.

BEING ACCOUNTABLE AND KEEPING TRACK OF YOUR ACTIVATES IS VERY IMPORTANT WHILE YOU ARE ON THIS JOURNEY. BECOMING A BOSS LADY IS HARD WORK, AND IT WILL NOT HAPPEN OVERNIGHT, BUT IT WILL HAPPEN. PLEASE JOURNAL THOUGHTS ABOUT THE ACTIVITIES YOU EXPERIENCE TODAY.

ACT LIKE A BOSS BY.....

RESEARCH– WHO'S YOUR FAVORITE BUSINESSWOMAN?

WHO IS SHE LYNN L. ELSENHANS? ☐ YES ☐ NO

WHAT DOES SHE DO?

WHAT IS HER NET WORTH? – $

WHAT INSPIRES YOU ABOUT HER?

MY GOAL FOR TODAY IS?

BOSSY THOUGHT:
I WILL GIVE BACK TO OTHERS.

BEING ACCOUNTABLE AND KEEPING TRACK OF YOUR ACTIVATES IS VERY IMPORTANT WHILE YOU ARE ON THIS JOURNEY. BECOMING A BOSS LADY IS HARD WORK, AND IT WILL NOT HAPPEN OVERNIGHT, BUT IT WILL HAPPEN. PLEASE JOURNAL THOUGHTS ABOUT THE ACTIVITIES YOU EXPERIENCE TODAY.

ACT LIKE A BOSS BY....

RESEARCH – WHO'S YOUR FAVORITE BUSINESS WOMAN?

WHO IS SHE BEYONCE KNOWLES? ☐ YES ☐ NO

WHAT DOES SHE DO?

WHAT IS HER NET WORTH? - $

WHAT INSPIRES YOU ABOUT HER?

MY GOAL FOR TODAY IS?

BOSSY THOUGHT:
I AM A SMART
BUSINESSWOMAN.

Being accountable and keeping track of your activates is very important while you are on this journey. Becoming a Boss Lady is hard work, and it will not happen overnight, but it will happen. Please journal thoughts about the activities you experience today.

____

____

____

____

____

____

____

____

____

____

____

____

____

____

____

____

____

____

____

____

____

____

____

____

____

____

____

> "SUCCESS COMES WITH A COST, AND YOU MUST PAY THE PRICE."

ACT LIKE A BOSS BY....

RESEARCH- WHO'S YOUR FAVORITE BUSINESS WOMAN?

WHO IS SHE TIFFNAY KRUMINS? ☐ YES ☐ NO
____

WHAT DOES SHE DO? ____

WHAT IS HER NET WORTH? - $ _______________________________________

WHAT INSPIRES YOU ABOUT HER? _____________________________________

MY GOAL FOR TODAY IS?

____

____

____

BOSSY THOUGHT:
I WILL INVEST IN MYSELF.

BEING ACCOUNTABLE AND KEEPING TRACK OF YOUR ACTIVATES IS VERY IMPORTANT WHILE YOU ARE ON THIS JOURNEY. BECOMING A BOSS LADY IS HARD WORK, AND IT WILL NOT HAPPEN OVERNIGHT, BUT IT WILL HAPPEN. PLEASE JOURNAL THOUGHTS ABOUT THE ACTIVITIES YOU EXPERIENCE TODAY.

ACT LIKE A BOSS BY....

RESEARCH – WHO'S YOUR FAVORITE BUSINESS WOMAN?

WHO IS SHE MARIE CALENDAR? ☐ YES ☐ NO

WHAT DOES SHE DO?

WHAT IS HER NET WORTH? - $

WHAT INSPIRES YOU ABOUT HER?

MY GOAL FOR TODAY IS?

BOSSY THOUGHT:
I AM UNSTOPPABLE.

Being accountable and keeping track of your activates is very important while you are on this journey. Becoming a Boss Lady is hard work, and it will not happen overnight, but it will happen. Please journal thoughts about the activities you experience today.

____

____

____

____

____

____

____

____

____

____

____

____

____

____

____

____

____

____

____

____

____

____

____

____

____

____

"FAILURE TO DECIDE ONLY MEANS DECISIONS WILL BE MADE FOR YOU."

ACT LIKE A BOSS BY....

RESEARCH – WHO'S YOUR FAVORITE BUSINESS WOMAN?

WHO IS SHE DEBBIE FIELDS? ☐ YES ☐ NO
____

WHAT DOES SHE DO?
____

WHAT IS HER NET WORTH? - $
____

WHAT INSPIRES YOU ABOUT HER?
____

MY GOAL FOR TODAY IS?

____

____

____

BOSSY THOUGHT:
I AM UNDENIABLE.

ACT LIKE A BOSS BY....

EDUCATION - ATTEND A SEMINAR THAT FOCUSES ON WOMEN ENTREPRENEURS

WHAT SEMINAR DID YOU ATTEND?

____

____

HOW WILL IT HELP YOUR JOURNEY?

____

____

MY GOAL FOR TODAY IS?

____

____

____

BOSSY THOUGHT:
FAILURE IS NOT AN OPTION FOR ME.

ACT LIKE A BOSS BY....

EDUCATION – Select your favorite womanpreneur to follow on social media

Who did you choose?

What is her business?

Check out: WWW.IFUNDWOMEN.COM

My goal for today is?

BOSSY THOUGHT:
I WILL NEVER, EVER GIVE UP ON MYSELF.

Being accountable and keeping track of your activates is very important while you are on this journey. Becoming a Boss Lady is hard work, and it will not happen overnight, but it will happen. Please journal thoughts about the activities you experience today.

ACT LIKE A BOSS BY....

PREPARATION- WRITE YOUR BUSINESS PLAN

USE THIS AS A ROAD MAP:

____

____

WRITE YOUR EXECUTIVE SUMMARY:

____

____

VISIT: **WWW.SCORE.ORG**

MY GOAL FOR TODAY IS?

____

____

____

BOSSY THOUGHT:
I WILL CELEBRATE OTHER'S SUCCESS.

Being accountable and keeping track of your activates is very important while you are on this journey. Becoming a Boss Lady is hard work, and it will not happen overnight, but it will happen. Please journal thoughts about the activities you experience today.

ACT LIKE A BOSS BY....

PREPARATION- VISIT: **WWW.EHOW.COM**

SEE IF YOUR TYPE OF BUSINESS CAN BE FOUND: ☐ YES ☐ NO

WRITE WHATEVER INFORMATION YOU FIND:

____

____

____

____

MY GOAL FOR TODAY IS?

____

____

____

BOSSY THOUGHT:
I AM NOT A SELFISH PERSON.

"C.E.O. Calculating Evaluating, Orchestrating."

Act Like A Boss By....

PREPARATION – Attend a seminar that focuses on women entrepreneurs.

What seminar did you attend?

How will it help your journey?

My goal for today is?

Bossy Thought:
I AM A GREAT PERSON.

Act Like A Boss By....

Legal – Decide on a business structure – compare their differences

Sole Proprietor–

LLC–

partnership–

My goal for today is?

Bossy Thought:
Fear has no place in my life.

Being accountable and keeping track of your activates is very important while you are on this journey. Becoming a Boss Lady is hard work, and it will not happen overnight, but it will happen. Please journal thoughts about the activities you experience today.

Act Like A Boss By....

LEGAL – Register the name (DBA)

What is the name of your business? _______________________

Describe the product or service you intend to provide.

____

____

____

My goal for today is?

____

____

____

Bossy Thought:
My faith will not waver.

Act Like A Boss By....

LEGAL— Apply for a tax id number
Visit: HTTPS://WWW.IRS.GOV/BUSINESSES

Record it here:

My goal for today is?

Bossy Thought:
I will stay focused.

BEING ACCOUNTABLE AND KEEPING TRACK OF YOUR ACTIVATES IS VERY IMPORTANT WHILE YOU ARE ON THIS JOURNEY. BECOMING A BOSS LADY IS HARD WORK, AND IT WILL NOT HAPPEN OVERNIGHT, BUT IT WILL HAPPEN. PLEASE JOURNAL THOUGHTS ABOUT THE ACTIVITIES YOU EXPERIENCE TODAY.

ACT LIKE A BOSS BY....

WEBSITE – DECIDE IF YOU WILL NEED A WEBSITE

CHECK OUT: **WWW.WIX.COM**

CHECK OUT: **WWW.GODADDY.COM**

MY GOAL FOR TODAY IS?

BOSSY THOUGHT:
I WILL NOT BE DISTRACTED.

Being accountable and keeping track of your activates is very important while you are on this journey. Becoming a Boss Lady is hard work, and it will not happen overnight, but it will happen. Please journal thoughts about the activities you experience today.

Act Like A Boss By....

WEBSITE- Do you need brochures?

What style would you like, bifold, trifold, quadfold, paper, or electronic?

BIFOLD	TRIFOLD	QUADFOLD
Yes ☐ No ☐	☐ Yes ☐ No	☐ Yes ☐ No

PAPER	ELECTRONIC
Yes ☐ No ☐	Yes ☐ No ☐

My goal for today is?

____

____

____

Bossy Thought:
I will be committed.

Being accountable and keeping track of your activates is very important while you are on this journey. Becoming a Boss Lady is hard work, and it will not happen overnight, but it will happen. Please journal thoughts about the activities you experience today.

____

____

____

____

____

____

____

____

____

____

____

____

____

____

____

____

____

____

____

____

____

____

____

ACT LIKE A BOSS BY....

WEBSITE- HIRE A WEB DESIGNER
CHECK OUT FIVERR.COM/S2/8AA6262C15   DONE ☐
CHECK OUT THUMTACK.COM   DONE ☐
CHECK OUT FREELANCE.COM   DONE ☐
CHECK OUT WIX.COM   DONE ☐

MY GOAL FOR TODAY IS?

____

____

____

BOSSY THOUGHT:
I SET REALISTIC GOALS.

Being accountable and keeping track of your activates is very important while you are on this journey. Becoming a Boss Lady is hard work, and it will not happen overnight, but it will happen. Please journal thoughts about the activities you experience today.

ACT LIKE A BOSS BY....

WEBSITE— ESTABLISH YOUR BUSINESS ON SOCIAL MEDIA

FACEBOOK NAME ___________

INSTAGRAM HANDLE ___________

LINKEDIN HANDLE ___________

MY GOAL FOR TODAY IS?

____

____

____

BOSSY THOUGHT:
I WILL GET ORGANIZED.

ACT LIKE A BOSS BY....

WEBSITE- INVITE YOUR FRIENDS AND FAMILY TO LIKE YOUR PAGE

HOW MANY LIKES CAN YOUR GET? _______________ FACEBOOK

HOW MANY LIKES CAN YOUR GET? _______________ INSTAGRAM

HOW MANY LIKES CAN YOUR GET? _______________ LINKEDIN

MY GOAL FOR TODAY IS?

____

____

____

BOSSY THOUGHT:
I AM A GREAT FOLLOWER.

ACT LIKE A BOSS BY....

WEBSITE— DO YOU NEED A LOGO?

WHAT IS YOUR COLOR SCHEME? _______________________________

WHAT TYPE OF LOGO DO YOU WANT ELEGANT, MODERN OR CLASSY?

____

MY GOAL FOR TODAY IS?

____

____

____

BOSSY THOUGHT:
I CAN DO ALL THINGS THROUGH CHRIST WHO STRENGTHENS ME.
(PHILIPPIANS 4:13)

Being accountable and keeping track of your activates is very important while you are on this journey. Becoming a Boss Lady is hard work, and it will not happen overnight, but it will happen. Please journal thoughts about the activities you experience today.

Act Like A Boss By....

WEBSITE- Do you need business cards?

What is your color scheme? _______________________________

What type of cards would you prefer, electronic or paper? _______________

Check out: WWW.VISTAPRINT.COM

My goal for today is?

____

____

____

Bossy Thought:
I AM A WINNER.

BEING ACCOUNTABLE AND KEEPING TRACK OF YOUR ACTIVATES IS VERY IMPORTANT WHILE YOU ARE ON THIS JOURNEY.
BECOMING A BOSS LADY IS HARD WORK, AND IT WILL NOT HAPPEN OVERNIGHT, BUT IT WILL HAPPEN. PLEASE
JOURNAL THOUGHTS ABOUT THE ACTIVITIES YOU EXPERIENCE TODAY.

Act Like A Boss By....

Financial's   Using your expense tracker on the opposite page

Record all fees including web hosting, ad cost, bank fees, etc.

My goal for today is?

____

____

____

Bossy Thought:
I will commit to learning new things.

Expense Tracker

Expense	Cost

Expense Tracker

Expense	Cost

Expense Tracker

Expense	Cost

ACT LIKE A BOSS BY....

FINANCIAL'S   CHECK OUT HTTPS://WWW.FUNDERA.COM/BLOG/SMALL-BUSINESS-GRANTS-FOR-WOMEN

JOIN THE SLACK COMMUNITY _______________________________________

OPEN A BUSINESS BANK ACCOUNT _______________________________

BRING YOUR DBA ____

TAX ID# ____

MY GOAL FOR TODAY IS?

____

____

____

BOSSY THOUGHT:
I AM CREDITWORTHY.

Being accountable and keeping track of your activates is very important while you are on this journey. Becoming a Boss Lady is hard work, and it will not happen overnight, but it will happen. Please journal thoughts about the activities you experience today.

Act Like A Boss By....

Financial's   Apply for a business credit card

Secure or not secure

Secure   ☐ Tick box that applies
Not secure   ☐ Tick box that applies

My goal for today is?

____

____

____

Bossy Thought:
I have integrity.

Act Like A Boss By.....

FINANCIAL'S   Do you need startup capital?

How much will you need?_______________________________

What will you use it for?_______________________________

____

Do you prefer credit or cash   ☐ Credit   ☐ Cash

My goal for today is?

____

____

____

Bossy Thought:
When life gets tough, I will get tougher.

BEING ACCOUNTABLE AND KEEPING TRACK OF YOUR ACTIVATES IS VERY IMPORTANT WHILE YOU ARE ON THIS JOURNEY. BECOMING A BOSS LADY IS HARD WORK, AND IT WILL NOT HAPPEN OVERNIGHT, BUT IT WILL HAPPEN. PLEASE JOURNAL THOUGHTS ABOUT THE ACTIVITIES YOU EXPERIENCE TODAY.

Act Like A Boss By....

Financial's   Open a business account

Try a secure business card with

Wells fargo, bbva compass or a credit union ______________________

____

____

My goal for today is?

____

____

____

Bossy Thought:
I will not crumble, I will conquer.

Being accountable and keeping track of your activates is very important while you are on this journey. Becoming a Boss Lady is hard work, and it will not happen overnight, but it will happen. Please journal thoughts about the activities you experience today.

Act Like A Boss By....

Financial's   Should you establish business credit?

Get a Dun & Bradstreet number _______________________

Visit: www.dnb.com
Visit: www.allbusiness.com

Are you a minority-owned business owner? _______________

Get certified visit: https://.nctrca.mwdbe.com _______________

My goal for today is?

____

____

____

Act Like A Boss By....

Financial's   Hire an accountant

Who did you hire? _______________________________________

Describe their experience. _______________________________
____

What do you like most about this accountant? _______________
____

My goal for today is?

____

____

____

Bossy Thought:
I will not let my dreams die.

____

____

____

____

____

____

____

____

____

____

____

____

____

____

____

____

____

____

____

____

____

____

____

____

____

____

Act Like A Boss By....

Financial's   Select an account software program to manage your accounting

Check out: quickbooks

Use this link for free trail - HTTPS://WWW.QUICKBOOKSOFFER.COM/?CID=IRP-4337#PRICING

My goal for today is?

____

____

____

Bossy Thought:
I am blessed and highly favored.

BEING ACCOUNTABLE AND KEEPING TRACK OF YOUR ACTIVATES IS VERY IMPORTANT WHILE YOU ARE ON THIS JOURNEY. BECOMING A BOSS LADY IS HARD WORK, AND IT WILL NOT HAPPEN OVERNIGHT, BUT IT WILL HAPPEN. PLEASE JOURNAL THOUGHTS ABOUT THE ACTIVITIES YOU EXPERIENCE TODAY.

ACT LIKE A BOSS BY....

FINANCIAL'S   DECIDE ON MARKETING BUDGET

HOW MUCH WILL YOU SPEND ON MARKETING/ADVERTISING? $

CHECK OUT FACEBOOK ADS $

CHECK OUT INSTAGRAM ADS $

MY GOAL FOR TODAY IS?

____

____

____

BOSSY THOUGHT:
I WILL NOT LIVE IN THE PAST.

Being accountable and keeping track of your activates is very important while you are on this journey. Becoming a Boss Lady is hard work, and it will not happen overnight, but it will happen. Please journal thoughts about the activities you experience today.

ACT LIKE A BOSS BY....

FINANCIAL'S   Consult with a tax preparer

HOW OFTEN DO YOU PLAN TO PAY YOUR TAXES?

QUARTERLY –

YEARLY –

MY GOAL FOR TODAY IS?

____

____

____

BOSSY THOUGHT:
I AM A CREATIVE PERSON.

BEING ACCOUNTABLE AND KEEPING TRACK OF YOUR ACTIVATES IS VERY IMPORTANT WHILE YOU ARE ON THIS JOURNEY. BECOMING A BOSS LADY IS HARD WORK, AND IT WILL NOT HAPPEN OVERNIGHT, BUT IT WILL HAPPEN. PLEASE JOURNAL THOUGHTS ABOUT THE ACTIVITIES YOU EXPERIENCE TODAY.

Extra Expense Tracker

Expense	Cost

Extra Expense Tracker

Expense	Cost

Extra Expense Tracker

Expense	Cost

Extra Expense Tracker

Expense	Cost

Extra Expense Tracker

Expense	Cost